THE STEAMING SIXTIES
Stirring episodes from the last decade of Steam on BR
7. The Southern Shore
Dorset, Devon and Cornwall
Seaside Branches of the Southern
By George Reeve

Copyright Irwell Press,
ISBN 978-1-906919-25-2
First published in 2010 by Irwell Press Ltd., 59A, High Street, Clophill, Bedfordshire, MK45 4BE
Printed by Konway Press.

The map of the Southern, or rather the South Western part of it, rather resembles a river flowing east, that dendritic, tree-like pattern that ends 'upstream' at its extremities in the west in branches, though 'twigs' are what some of its farthest reaches call to mind. In winter a South Western branch to the seaside might be a branch like any other yet, especially in summer, they became linked directly to London, as a sequence of expresses were timed to make a succession of main line connections, dropping off coaches in an intricate system that would be wholly impossible with the stock, low staffing levels and simplified layouts we have now. Not to mention the closed and lifted branches! This access to the capital worked like a well oiled machine. You could board a coach at your local sleepy station, amid fields, hedgerows and twittering birds and expect next to be in London, more than 200 miles away. It derived of course from the West Country and its singular attraction to Britain's growing army of holidaymakers. It was what historians called the 'seaside holiday habit' (making it appear slightly disreputable) and they came not just from London but from the Midlands and the North. In a direct through coach your bulging suitcase, hoisted with a sigh of regret (or maybe not, given the weather)

into the luggage rack within sight and sound of seagulls and the sea, didn't move till the slamming of doors and the steam and smoke of Waterloo. A perfect system!

My thanks to Mike King, Peter Swift, Ivan Smith and Eric Youldon for reading and contributing to the proof. To Nick Pomfret for helping with the slides and finally my sincere thanks to the South Western Circle for making available the slides from the George Powell and John Eyers collections without which this book would not have been possible.

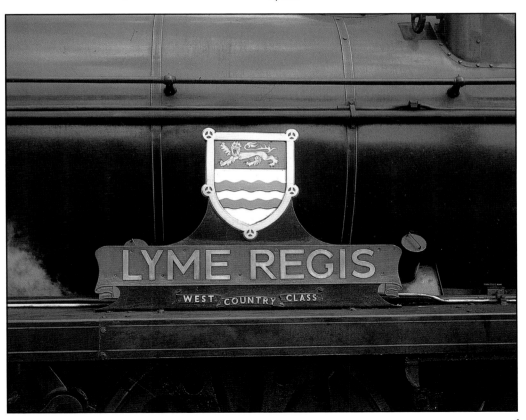

Cover. Adams Radial 4-4-2T taking water on the up main at Axminster station, 23 July 1960. See also page 22. George Powell.

Below. LYME REGIS at Salisbury, 1963. John Eyers.

Salisbury around 1964 with BR Standard 4MT 2-6-0 76016 on a Portsmouth-Cardiff train. The class had come to the fore on Southern cross-country working as the older types went to the wall and were to be found everywhere on passenger work this late on, to an extent probably not known anywhere else in the country. The stock comprises BR MkI 3-set 558 strengthened to seven coaches with Bulleid vehicles specifically for this working. Note also the roof-boards above the passenger compartments of the leading coach. John Eyers.

A filthy 34024 TAMAR VALLEY at Templecombe on the main line, 8 September 1961 with an up train of very mixed stock comprising a Southern 'utility' van, GWR Fruit D van, BR MkI 3-set plus Bulleid coaches on the rear. The girders mark bridge no.326 over the road to Wincanton away to the north, to the right. The station had been rebuilt by the Southern before the war, in 1937-38; this resulted in this familiar style of awning and so on, while the station building was recreated in a thoroughly art deco style, giving the place the air of the South London suburbs. George Powell.

Templecombe again, this time with a Merchant Navy, 35025 BROCKLEBANK LINE on a down train for Exeter, at the west end of the station. The day is the same as the previous view, 8 September 1961. An unlikely target, for it was a remote country junction after all, it was in fact bombed during the Second World War, in September 1942. It was deemed a target during fighter-bomber raids throughout the dangerous summer of 1942, conducted by small flights which dodged radar and could turn up literally out of the blue, to murderous effect. George Powell.

A way further down the main line was the little wayside station of Milborne Port Halt; possibly no other 'port' in the country lay further from open water, while its citizens were mainly occupied in the production of gloves. The charming signalbox, dozing as usual on 7 September 1961, was responsible for the crossovers at either end and though it might look sleepy enough, trains thundered through at 85mph, the maximum permitted speed for the main line. The box closed at midnight and didn't reopen till 5 in the morning; as the sign indicates, those very few passengers who found the sparse service useful obtained tickets from the signalman, who was actually a porter/signalman. George Powell.

Milborne Port Halt again on 7 September 1961; the stationmasters house had appeared in 1860. The view is towards Sherborne and shows the goods yard most conveniently served by down freights. Any traffic from the west had to circulate back via Templecombe. The box in fact played a more important role in the traffic of the line than the station; only a handful of passengers ever appeared but the box was vital in speeding traffic along between Templecombe and Sherborne. When Milborne box was switched out at night for instance Templecombe had to accept trains from Sherborne, which was more than six miles away. George Powell.

Sherborne on 8 September 1961, with 34072 257 SQUADRON on an up train. It was one of the largest towns on the main line and generated plenty of traffic, not least from the local public schools, Sherborne and Sherborne Girls. In *Main Line to the West, Part Two Salisbury to Yeovil* (Irwell Press 2007) we describe the procedures, unimaginable today, whereby each House Matron would acquaint herself with her girls' requirements and present a list to the Booking Office. All very Searlesque... George Powell.

A freight clanks in behind U mogul 31632 on 8 September 1961, photographed from the down platform. The shunt signal is off (visible beyond the train) suggesting the mogul is about to set back into the goods yard. Note also the lack of any headcode disks. This nearest awning, an arc roof to the down waiting rooms which was merely extended out had been gently decaying for years but by the time of this view had been replaced (earlier in the same year, 1961, indeed) by a more modern glass and steel structure. George Powell.

King Arthur 4-6-0 30799 SIR IRONSIDE with an up train on 8 September 1961 comprising a BR standard 3-set, still in carmine and cream. Sherborne had a level crossing (at the east end, behind the photographer) from the first; all trains stopped so the cost of a bridge was not thought worthwhile. Trains inevitably began to run through and at speed as often as not, for there was a stiffish climb to Milborne Port and drivers naturally wanted a good run at it. This provoked some nervous concern in the town at various periods. From 1964 operations reverted to the original pattern of the 1850s, with all trains stopping here, at what is now one of the busiest stations on the line. The girdering marks the hidden waters of the River Yeo, running under the station at this point. George Powell.

Sherborne up platform again, this time with 34079 141 SQUADRON, on 8 September 1961, with a stopper from Exeter and BR MkI stock set 522. The Pacific had come from the Eastern Section, having spent its first decade at Ramsgate; it had gone to Exmouth Junction in 1958 and eventually washed up at Eastleigh for its last couple of years with the demise of steam in the West and the end of Exmouth Junction shed. George Powell.

Merchant Navy 35001 CHANNEL PACKET leaves Sherborne with a down train for Exeter, 8 September 1961. The goods yard, loading dock and goods shed were over on the left, but there were also a bay line and a down siding (protected by that sand drag, with the trolley parked out of use) which ran down to a wagon turntable – it's that line disappearing to the right. In a marvellous confection for a model layout, a stub siding ran off the wagon turntable across a bridge over the River Yeo to the old gas works; two or three wagons of coal were taken down there every day – by the trip engine presumably – and then manhandled by pinch bar aided by a horse. Sadly by the time of this view the gas works (which pre-dated the coming of the railway by decades) had finally closed. From 1957 the town had been supplied from the national system but the grand offices survived, at least until recently, as residential accommodation. George Powell.

Next down the line from Sherborne came Yeovil Junction; Yeovil itself remained one of those rarities on our lines, a town connected to its main line by a branch shuttle, though there were through trains from Yeovil Town to London/Exeter too. So it was that, 'outwith the city walls' as it were, Yeovil Junction despite a remote location, grew to be amongst the biggest stations on the line, with these magnificent four tracks through the middle of it. It had long been a mean, cramped affair, a building mainly in wood which had seen a better century, let alone better days, when the LSWR rebuilt the whole place in this expansive style, a job completed in 1909. There were *two miles* of sidings for instance, together with a locomotive turntable (enlarged after the Second World War) and still in use for steam workings. Light Pacific 34086 219 SQUADRON is on an up three coach local stopping train, formed of a Bulleid composite flanked by the BR MkI brakes, a temporary formation for set 531, on 8 September 1961. Many of these LSW stations in the west had features that were just, well, out of the ordinary; running left to right (that is, south to north) deep under these running lines was an enormously lengthy 'cattle subway'. One shudders at the thought of conditions down there; you'd never complain about the London Tube again. And did any other company put magnificent nameboards like that on the gable ends of their awnings? George Powell.

M7 0-4-4T 30131, a Yeovil engine since 1951 and a stalwart on the Yeovil Town-Yeovil Junction pull-push trains, approaches the up platform at Yeovil Junction on 8 September 1961 with the branch train and a through coach from Yeovil Town. This, and the next two photos, show a shunting sequence similar to that performed at many Southern stations across the west of England. A train, the 8.55 Ilfracombe to Salisbury

comprising a Bulleid 3 coach set 770 series, has arrived at Yeovil Junction at 12.42. It was an all stations stopper and had picked up a through coach from the Lyme Regis branch at Axminster. Another through coach, from Yeovil Town and shown in this sequence, is being propelled by 30131 onto the back of the recently arrived Ilfracombe train. The five coaches now left for Salisbury where further shunting was performed. On arrival at Salisbury the two through coaches were detached from the Ilfracombe stopper and shunted onto the Atlantic Coast Express, which had left Padstow at 9.35. The train now left for London arriving at Waterloo at 3.32. George Powell.

The train for Salisbury has left to leave the branch train to move slowly forward along the up platform to reverse back into the branch loop, there being insufficient space for the train to reverse via the run-round at the western end. The utility van, 1996, was one of the five former SECR vans equipped with through pipes for push pull working. George Powell.

Salisbury's BR 4MT 2-6-0 76008 with an up train at Chard Junction, another station remote from the town and connected by a branch, around 1962. The branch bay was some yards off, behind the station building and led away north for a mile or two to the town itself. The branch and station closed in 1966. George Powell.

A pleasant summer day at Chard Junction, looking east in 1962. The main traffic was milk; the creamery was over on the right and one of the tankers which were always to be seen here sits in the bay on the left. Milk for the Wiltshire United Dairies was all that remained after the station closed in 1966. From *Main Line to the West Part Three Yeovil to Exeter* (Irwell Press 2009): 'The heavy milk traffic continued and although all other railway staff had been made redundant the signalmen were still required for the level crossing and milk sidings. So when the Western Region decided to single the main line the signal box here was retained to operate a long passing loop, the line to Sherborne being reduced to a single track on 7 May 1967 and to Honiton on 11 June 1967. The former up line was signalled for two way working. The original 1875 South Western signal box remained in use until September 1982 when it was replaced by a modern box. In a tacit admission of the futility of singling the line the Western Region now had to send milk trains from Chard Junction to London via Exeter, adding another 60 miles to the journey. Although the dairy remains in business and the sidings are intact, sadly no milk traffic has run by rail since 1980.' George Powell.

Along the line again and 35017 BELGIAN MARINE pauses at Axminster with what appears to be the down Atlantic Coast Express 1 August 1962. The weekday *ACE* did not usually call here but of course summer Saturdays might be very different. The lovely old place was looking decidedly down at heel by this time but was soon to receive a new lick of paint (see page 26) which cheered it up no end. The signal box was one of those splendid frugal affairs of standard period origin – a timber structure raised up on a stone base which could be equally executed in brick. Coaches here would be shunted off the rear of the train to the up bay by the branch loco ready for the short journey to Lyme Regis. George Powell.

Another mid-week summer train sets off for the west on 1 August 1962 behind 35001 CHANNEL PACKET, last seen at Sherborne. Often (though this was more typical of a summer Saturday perhaps) both up and down trains called, connecting with the branch train at the same time, waiting in the bay at the left. On such occasions the up platform would be crowded with holidaymakers. The train comprises typical mixed stock - a loose Maunsell coach, then a BR 3-set, another Maunsell followed by Bulleids. George Powell.

The prospect west from Axminster on 23 July 1960. The Lyme Regis bay line and its run-round loop trail off to the right and the branch itself curves away from the main line before swinging to the south to cross the main line by the modest flyover crossing the main line, visible in the distance. George Powell.

Axminster - change for Lyme Regis. Adams Radial 4-4-2T 30582 waits patiently in the bay platform ready for the short journey to Lyme Regis on 23 July 1960. The Radials came to the branch in 1913 and despite attempts to find alternatives they came to dominate proceedings on the line until the 1960s. The run round loop and platform were badly configured at Axminster and required some shunting movements before the train was ready for the return trip. 30582 would have drawn the branch train into the platform to allow the passengers off and then propelled the train back freeing the points for the runround. Once coupled the locomotive would propel the coaches back into the platform, as here. George Powell.

On the same day sister 30583 was taking water on the up main – a companion to the picture on the cover. It is a bit grubby and 30582 is sparkling by comparison; an explanation might lie in the fact that 30582 had received a general overhaul in June the previous year whilst 30583 had received hers in early 1959. With their ancient lineage it is not surprising therefore that the two were eventually condemned and sent to Eastleigh in July 1961, 30582, the most recently serviced, was saved from the cutters torch and thankfully went to the Bluebell Railway. This was a Saturday when the Adams tanks went to Exmouth Junction for washout and minor servicing to be replaced by another; watered up, 30583 would be ready to return to Exeter as possibly pilot to a down stopper. The branch was basically a one engine job but at peak times, during the summer months, a second would appear to help out with the heavier loads most notably on double headed trains. George Powell.

The third Radial, 30584, at Axminster on Saturday July 17 1960. As mentioned previously, at peak summer times, two of the three Radials could be found on the branch. 30584 is a bit grimy too and had received only an intermediate service at Eastleigh in May 1958. George Powell.

Above and right. The Radial has brought in the branch set, which is parked in the bay to the right, and is shunting a Bulleid through carriage across from a down train (probably from the Atlantic Coast Express) and will attach it to the branch set for the journey to Lyme Regis. In the right hand view the coach is now attached to the regular branch Set 108, which was formed of SR Maunsell corridor brake composite and an SECR non-corridor 10 -compartment second, and will soon depart for the coast. Both George Powell.

Axminster in the summer of 1963, newly repainted (water columns, seats, bridge – everything) in that lovely (though not quite LSW) pastel green and cream, still so redolent of the South West lines and of English summers; the chimney for the water tank pump, a bit doddery for years, has been removed. Lyme Regis bay with its water tank and column to the left, down platform extended under the bridge in that curious and distinctive way. It's still there like that and it is instructive to walk along and experience just how restricted it was under there. That far part is not now largely out of use, and the various concrete survivals, posts and so on, can take your mind back to days like this. George Powell.

Combpyne and a clouded sky, 23 July 1960. It had been 'Combpyne for the Landslip' until the Second World War when its signs were removed to confuse any invading German forces. The photographer is standing on the platform; the bare ballast marks the old crossing loop, now long removed. Axminster lies in the distance; behind us the line continues on to Lyme. The siding was kept for this camping coach, long an institution at this remote place. It's number was 38 and it was formerly lavatory composite SR5056 and once ran in set 253. It is barely possible to even imagine such holidays today; without a car and water delivered in old milk churns. And you probably had to walk across to the station building for the loo. The camping coach is number 38, formerly lavatory composite SR5056, and once formed in 3/4 set 253. George Powell.

Combpyne station building the same day; point lever on the camping coach siding in foreground, Lyme to left; this was more or less the summit of the line, at nearly 500 feet above sea level. The single storey building fronting the road was the waiting room and ticket office but almost the only passengers would be walkers in the summer or the handful of schoolchildren/shoppers that this sparsely populated district of fields and farms could muster. George Powell.

Looking down the leafy station approach to the town at Lyme Regis, 23 July 1960. It was called 'Lyme Regis for Charmouth' until the boards were removed in the war (the area was the front line after all) and reinstated simply as Lyme Regis. The station building, signal box and goods shed were all built in wood; this practical little structure has now been reconstituted as a most pleasant cafe on the Watercress Line in Hampshire. George Powell.

The station building at the head of the station approach. It was a short but stiff walk out of the town though this of course was from the higher bits of steeply graded Lyme – from the beach it was a mile away with a climb of some 250 feet! George Powell.

The station with its little signalbox at the far end of the platform. The platforms were lengthened and given new coping around 1930 (at the same time as Combpyne was altered to a single platform face). This is not the station building in its original form of 1903; in the period before nationalisation the Southern had carried out alterations which saw the building lengthened in anticipation of a restoration to 1930s traffic levels. The old, mouldering flat roof was replaced by the more conventional one we see here. George Powell.

Radial 30583 shunting some wagons past the curious wooden goods shed; it provided overnight accommodation, would you believe, for early turn crews on summer weekends. They camped out in a cabin attached to one end. The town was of course perfect for a pint and a fish and chip supper. George Powell.

The engine shed, at the extremity of the layout as the single line took off for the gorse-clad slopes and woods beyond. By the end of the war the little building was all but falling down but it was refurbished in spare asbestos corrugated sheeting, left over from other jobs, in 1947. The elderly frame and further shifting of the supporting dwarf wall however could not disguise a somewhat precarious look. For such a sleepy place it saw some desperate times – it had originally been in wood and twice as long but burnt down within three or four years of the opening of the line. Locomotives stood in the open until this replacement appeared just before the Great War. George Powell.

30583 had been the one to be rescued, derelict in 1946, from the East Kent Railway and restored at Eastleigh for use on the branch. Two Radials were insufficient for the peaks and O2 0-4-4Ts, which had to act as substitutes, were not perfect for the work. Duly repaired the 'new' Radial entered traffic as one of what was now the Lyme Regis trio; it became an unlikely survivor, rescued by the Bluebell Railway while the other two were broken up in 1961-62. George Powell.

30584 outside the shed on 23 July 1960. D.L. Bradley in his history of LSWR classes called this the 'worst Radial' meaning of course it was long overdue for an overhaul (they were all getting a bit doddery) and it was withdrawn in January 1961, after Ivatt 2-6-2Ts were cleared to work on the line *in extremis* – see over. George Powell.

30582 ready for the run back to Axminster. With the Radials approaching the end of their natural, thought was given to replacements and as far back as late 1958 a WR 0-4-2T was tried, though it proved inadequate. Over much of 1961 an extensive programme of track renewal meant that the Ivatt 2-6-2Ts could be tried for the first time, and 41297 from Barnstaple was tested, first for clearances and then on two coaches. It was deemed that the Ivatts could be used in time of need as noted earlier, though later in the year 41308 was tried out on trains up to six coaches, and seemed to perform well enough. After withdrawal of the last two Radials in 1961, Ivatt tanks took over until DMUs arrived in late 1963. However, a shortage of units in early 1965 saw a temporary return of the Ivatt 2-6-2Ts. The use of push-pull 'Gate' set 373 is interesting as this operation was never used on the branch. The LSWR 'Gate stock' were more generally associated with services on the Plymouth-Turnchapel and Weymouth-Portland lines although 373 did wander around a bit and was in its last years being withdrawn in October 1960. George Powell.

Seaton Junction and its remarkable concrete footbridge (the most expansive example of the Exmouth Junction concrete arts) looking east in August 1961. It is not often appreciated just how considerable was the investment by the Southern in its western outposts. A fortune was spent on new buildings and layouts. It was serious stuff and the SR Board put its money where its mouth was – unpromising areas included the Lynton and Barnstaple and the Isle of Wight. It was surely a scurrilous rumour that the coast was chosen for the more agreeable opportunities it offered for tours of inspection by the Directors and Officers! Standing in the down local is S15 4-6-0 30823; to the right is the curving Seaton branch platform and that long bridge carrying a footpath over the line. It did not serve the platforms; that was done by the station footbridge just visible beyond. On the left is the extensive and important premises of the Express Dairy Co. George Powell.

34109 SIR TRAFFORD LEIGH-MALLORY light at Seaton Junction in August 1961. The fact 34109 is here light engine, and carries west of England route discs, may suggest that it had failed and has had to be replaced. A more likely senario however, is that it has brought a combined Lyme Regis/Seaton train as far as here and will then run light to Exmouth Junction. George Powell.

Looking west from Seaton Junction in August 1961 and the advance starting signal set for a train on the down through line with LSWR lower quadrant arms. Seaton Junction had opened as 'Colyton' in 1860; the branch and the name change followed in 1869. The layout, reminiscent of Yeovil Junction with four tracks through the station had come about after another of the Southern's bold rebuilding/widening projects, carried out over 1927-28. George Powell is almost standing on the branch line whilst the track running off to the left is a siding. The milk tanks, on the other side of the line, were an ever-present feature at Seaton Junction. Ahead lie the rigours of Honiton bank. George Powell.

Seaton Junction looking east and the elegant tall signal, with co-acting repeater, gives the all clear for a train in the up local. Why it was felt necessary for a tall arm to be installed for the platform road is not clear. George Powell.

Parked in the siding on the down side, west end, at Seaton Junction are push-pull set No.1 in its post-July1958 form of LSWR driving brake composite 6488 and SECR 10 compartment second 1066. Behind are some milk tanks from the Express dairy which was sited on the up side of the station. George Powell.

Colyton on the Seaton branch in August 1961. A typical hybrid station with original stationmaster's house and waiting/booking rooms, together with later concrete panel fencing and that peculiar brick hut with sliding doors which was used as a goods store. The station and line closed in March 1966, but now forms the northern terminus of the Seaton Tramway. George Powell.

Seaton and the wonderful 'art deco' frontage which appeared on the rebuilding of the station in 1937 and bringing, one might say, a touch of Southern suburbia to East Devon. It wasn't a cosmetic rebuilding but a whole-sale reconstruction of the station site, similar to the work carried out at Seaton Junction some years earlier. Away went the cluttered original Seaton and Beer station building, small wooden engine shed and short platforms, to be replaced by this splendid frontage, concrete engine shed and excursion length paltforms. My mother and sister were evacuated here in 1940 and remember only too well the hoards of people passing through the little gateway to a life of relative safety after the terrors of night bombing in London. It would be short lived, however, as they ventured further west to be near my father stationed in Plymouth and later Bude. George Powell.

Sidmouth Junction and the view westward from the footbridge at the west end of the station. In September 1960 a rake of Meldon stone arrives behind a not-long-for-this-world Maunsell Arthur 30450 SIR KAY which has lost its Drummond tender receiving the Urie tender from withdrawn Arthur 30737 in October 1956. This may well be the 1.55pm from Meldon, arrival due 4.5pm. SIR KAY will probably be replaced by another loco after the train is set back into the up siding before continuing to Salisbury. George Powell.

They come out best on
Kodak film

The railway in its glorious Devon landscape; this is the prospect east from that Sidmouth Junction footbridge again, in September 1960. A Merchant Navy is thundering down with an express for Exeter, passing an Ivatt 2-6-2T destined for the branch; this curves away to the right and, with the eye of faith, you might just make out another loco coming in with the branch train. George Powell.

A last look from that footbridge, the gates closing as the Merchant Navy which has swept through on the last part of its journey to Exeter. By now the LSWR lattice signal, lower quadrant arms have been replced by BR upper quadrants, but the up home, visible beyond, retains its lower quadrant arm together with visibility shield. George Powell.

A pause at Exeter Central about 1963/64 before we take off for the north, to admire 34096 TREVONE, not long rebuilt. It was another Ramsgate refugee, coming to Exmouth Junction in 1958. In the background is a Derby built 3-car DMU (later class 116) and beyond that is a set of BR standard non-corridor carriages which had previously been used on the Exeter-Exmouth services. George Powell.

Barnstaple Town from the rear of a DMU (note the signals for down train at clear). This is the minor level crossing, looking towards Barnstaple Junction past the little signalbox. The loop to the right was removed a while before. During the summer of 1964, North Devon line trains with through carriages from Waterloo were worked by Hymeks and NBL Type 2s. Heavy trains needed banking by an N class on the approach to Mortehoe in either direction. DMUs were only on services which started from Exeter. John Eyers

The Atlantic Coast at last, and a remarkable photograph. This is September 1963, the last full year of steam and 34081 92 SQUADRON (the rebuilt Pacifics were barred from lines such as this, which was as good a reason as any not to convert any more of them) exits the terminus. Perched high above the town the line seemed to cling to the heights whenever it could. The mighty Atlantic (well, let's face it, the Bristol Channel) looking blue for once rather than brown, stretches away on the horizon. The whole composition is exquisite, not least for the inclusion of the perfectly self-contained single road engine shed (the similar building at Okehampton comes to mind) its site carved out of the living rock in yet another of the Southern's bold and committed investments in the West. Immediately in front of the shed, out of sight below the pines, was a 70ft turntable which could turn the largest engines used on the line. John Eyers.

92 SQUADRON disappears round the curve out of Ilfracombe above the little hamlets of Higher and Lower Slade. This was a local as far as Exeter but it is extraordinary now to recall that every day, from so many remote country outposts, you could settle in your seat and not have to wake up (though you'd have to be a true Philistine) until the ranks of terraces around Clapham Junction – enough time for a stretch and a yawn before coming to stand in Waterloo. From this – to there... John Eyers.

This is Okehampton around 1960-61 with a T9 4-4-0 in the Bude bay; the view is west of course, and a light Pacific fusses away in the 'military siding' on the up side. The remnants of this place are fascinatingly still there; the sidings originated as an embarkation point for troops at Okehampton Camp and finished life as the loading/unloading point for the short-lived (1960-64) Surbiton-Okehampton car carrier trains. Like so many places along this remarkable line, Okehampton station somehow clung to the hillside – on the right is the distant horizon and some indication of the slope falling away to the town below. George Powell.

Dunsland Cross ('Alight here for Shebbear College') on the Bude line, 23 September 1964. We are very much in 'Withered Arm' territory now, where you'd have to wonder just *where* would passengers come from? Did they merely emerge from the bushes? Yet out of the mists through this wild lonely country (though I wouldn't want to get too *Hound of the Baskervilles* about this) would come, magnificent even with only three coaches, the Atlantic Coast Express with WATERLOO on its destination boards! The station wasn't alone in its isolation in the West of course and, naturally, the college was miles away. George Powell.

Holsworthy on 23 September 1964, final days of the Atlantic Coast Express. This was at first the terminus of the line, rather than Bude and when completed in 1879 it had its own little engine shed and turntable for the branch locomotive. This original platform had been constructed in stone whilst the later addition of a loop platform, when the line was extended to Bude, was executed in brick. We are looking towards Halwill Junction and the magnificent Holsworthy East Viaduct, out of view, a structure still there today but obsured by vegetation and buildings. A splendid station, also still with us, perched on the side of a hill (nothing discouraged our Victorian forebears) the writing was very much on the wall by now. It would never be this good again. George Powell.

Holsworthy on the same occasion as the previous view. The curious figure of authority in cap, armband and wellies receiving a tugged forelock, was a *Western Region* PW Foreman; another portent of things to come. Apart from HM Forces and the Police the British, I sometimes feel (lets add nurses) never really mastered uniform... This newer platform and the signal box opened in 1898. The box was of the LSWR central pillar variety; the 20-lever frame included one for the up advanced starter, more than a quarter of a mile away! George Powell.

The down loop at Holsworthy, 23 September 1964, with one of the BR 4MT 2-6-4Ts, and BR set 3-set 890 (ex 4-set), which appeared in the last year or two of steam. Closure notices for the Bude line and the North Cornwall line had in fact already been issued, in April, with closure scheduled for October but vigorous protests delayed the end till 1966. Operational costs of the lines Okehampton-Bude and Halwill-Wadebridge, both single track steam lines, was put at £150,000 a year, against income of only about £40,000. The Atlantic Coast Express running in the week with three coaches behind a light Pacific in original condition (with added filth) was said on weekdays to be populated by railwaymen and schoolchildren and very few passengers paying the normal fare. John Eyers.

Holsworthy finally closed with the line on 1 October 1966; here it is more or less intact on 6 July 1965. The 'reprieve' merely meant, you suspect, an even more miserable and unattractive service than ever for the last years. In truth the pattern of services, especially in winter, remained unaltered for years, a product of inertia and the restrictions of single track working. It was all good enough until buses and cars were available, then the public deserted the straggling lines of the Withered Arm. The perceived jackboot (or should that be wellies – see page 54) of the Western Region, taking over the lines from January 1963 with the deliberate intent of closing them all, didn't make the pill any easier to swallow however. John Eyers.

One of the original batch of nine Standard 2-6-4Ts delivered to Exmouth Junction in 1962, 80041 at Whitstone and Bridgerule, with a train for Halwill Junction on 23 September 1964. Twelve of the BR 4MT 2-6-4Ts eventually came to Exmouth Junction in 1962, made redundant by electrification and closures in Kent. They offered some stiffening for the Bude services following the demise of the 4-4-0s on the North Cornwall lines, principally a tender engine domain. Bude shed closed in September 1964, the men being made redundant although servicing facilities remained into 1965. The loco carries the headcode for Okehampton to Padstow, the Bude branch requiring a single disk on the nearside. However, in an area where everyone knew where the trains were going one has to say so what! John Eyers.

Bude station on 23 September 1964. Bude was a mere speck smelling of fish and deemed unworthy of a railway when the line opened to Holsworthy in 1879 but it grew and flourished in the way that so many Victorian resorts did and it eventually got the line it desired in 1898. So the station was suitably elegant, with a stationmasters house at one end, a fine high slated roof, high quality brick and stone and every attention to detail. As mentioned earlier, my mother and sister came to Bude, via a fourteen hour rail trip from Seaton, in March 1941 at the end of a very cold winter and were housed in the Links Hotel, a small establishment opposite the magnificent Bude golf course. The bombing in Plymouth had been intense since the early part of 1941 so my father's transfer to Bude, to man an anti-aircraft battery, came as some relief to my mother. He was billeted in the Royal British Legion accommodation two doors up from the Links Hotel which she recalled as being 'very convenient'. This convenience was not to last long however, with my father's unit joining the newly formed 8th Army in September 1941 and seeing action on the sands of North Africa almost immediately in November 1941 - she did not see him again until demob in 1946. John Eyers.

The Bude platform. It was at the edge of town (a result no doubt of arriving so late) and by this time, September 1964, was deserted more often than not. Those trolleys sadly won't see much more work, you feel. Off the platform end is the little one road engine shed and its water tank, its roof having rotted away some years before. The line to the wharf ran off to the right behind the shed; rising in the background is the gasworks. John Eyers.

Some Cornish scraps now, beginning with one of the Beattie well tanks, 30585, taking water at Pencarrow Woods on the Wenford line in August 1961. The railway to Wenford Bridge was very much part of the landscape – part of the vegetation almost. It 'lived off the land' and the water supply here came from a spring, diverted upslope and channelled in troughing to the 'tank' here. The 1366 pannier tanks which replaced the well tanks took the best part of an hour to fill their tanks but they were higher than the 2-4-0Ts – they presumably only took half an hour or so. George Powell.

Dunmere Junction in September 1961. One can imagine the pleasure spent watching train movements onto the branch from that garden wall on a balmy summers evening, although I must confess it would hardly have resembled the train movements of Clapham Junction. Maybe sitting there with a glass of home made lemonade and a piece of mum's fruit cake. The train from Wadebridge, over four miles away, has entered the branch through the gate in the distance which marked the point the Wenford Bridge Branch of the Bodmin & Wadebridge Railway diverged to Bodmin. George Powell.

Dunmere Junction and the gate now behind us and the daily freight disappearing into the distance and onwards to Wenford Bridge itself. George Powell.

Wadebridge about 1960 with that tall lattice starter signal, SR concrete lamp post, LSWR water column and 'fire devil' to keep its water flowing in the frost. The view is an unusual one, to furthest Cornwall and the terminus of the North Cornwall, Padstow. The footbridge in the distance allows pedestrians to cross when the Molesworth Street level was closed and in the summer months the cause of congestion to rival Honiton at its very worse. Various ancient buildings of the old Bodmin & Wadebridge survive there. The 'main line' ran down a very restricted strip of ground between a footpath and a road before crossing Molesworth Street and of the many wonders of the journey, passengers had an intimate view of not the least of them, a wet fish shop, as the train inched its way over the crossing. George Powell.

End of the line; Padstow 259miles 57 chains from Waterloo - well not the station but the buffers at the end of the jetty some 300 yards away behind the loco. The Southern's furthest point and an apt place for some ancient loco types to see out their days. T9 30712 waiting to depart with the 3.13pm train to Wadebridge. George Powell.